T0113503

FOR ALL
EYES ONLY

BUNNY HERSCHENSOHN

authorHOUSE®

AuthorHouse™
1663 Liberty Drive
Bloomington, IN 47403
www.authorhouse.com
Phone: 833-262-8899

Published by AuthorHouse 09/11/2020

ISBN: 978-1-7283-7060-6 (sc)
ISBN: 978-1-7283-7250-1 (e)

Library of Congress Control Number: 2020916587

Print information available on the last page.

Any people depicted in stock imagery provided by Getty Images are models, and such images are being used for illustrative purposes only.
Certain stock imagery © Getty Images.

This book is printed on acid-free paper.

CONTENTS

ACKNOWLEDGEMENTS

I'm dedicating this book "FOR ALL EYES ONLY" to 3 awesome families…the Domenic Family the Manuel Family and the Herschensohn Family; all of whom have meant the world to me and all of whom I will love and cherish… forever.

I also want to give a big shout-out to Sonny Lee; a gentle and good man who deserves the best of everything life has to offer.

FOREWORD

Prior to Covid-19 our basic liberties including our Judeo-Christian values were being banned and/or replaced methodically. Then and now fear, hatred, intimidation, vengeance and anxiety permeate our social and political landscape. It is through this radical fundamental transformation agenda that our Republic, a Constitutional free market system of governing, can evolve into a Socialist government controlled system.

Today, we are fighting two wars simultaneously... the Coronavirus Pandemic and the radical Progressive Democrats. Both are drastically altering our lifestyles but not for the same reasons. Covid-19 has led to an enforced *temporary* nation-wide shut-down due to life and death unprecedented health circumstances. The radical Progressive Democrats are taking advantage of this crisis to shut us down *permanently* by enacting their radical fundamental transformation agenda through *anarchy*. Orchestrated chaos can destroy any country. Hence, we must become more vigilant than ever since this Pandemic could be the

"Perfect Storm" that enables the "Perfect Crime" to come into fruition. In order for Socialism to exist; individual freedoms must desist. Therefore, don't take your eye off the political ball. REJECT and RESIST losing our civil liberties during this complex dilemma.

Perhaps revisiting some of the problematic issues via a *TIMELINE OF BLOGS* written during the "*Fundamental Transformation*" era of the Obama Administration can shed some light on just how a few of the disheartening ills and unrest we face today were actually created and enacted upon one by one... through academia, social engineering, legislation, political rhetoric, and slick deception and deceit. And maybe these flagrant "red flags" from yesteryear can now make it easier to identify and prevent any future attempts to obliterate America from the ground up.*

POLITICALLY CORRECT OR POLITICAL SUICIDE

By Bunny Herschensohn   **JUNE 12, 2012**

The *"Free Dictionary"* defines *"Politically Correct"* as conforming to a particular sociopolitical ideology or point of view, especially to a liberal point of view; regarding behavior. The interesting revelation here signifies that "Politically Correct" has a liberal point of view. Hence, this is especially problematic since the **Progressive Democrat Party owns Politically Correct and uses it exclusively to enforce "absolute" behavioral laws to subjective situations without justification, precedence, debate or consequences.** PC dictates the solution to every conceivable problem, and picks winners and losers according to the content that most fits the liberal narrative. The best part is: **NO ONE IS HELD ACCOUNTABLE.** How apropos and convenient is that minor detail? Our citizens have been victimized relentlessly by these one-sided intangible **Politically Correct Reformations.**

It is now "**politically correct**" to *remove* a Nativity Scene, a Christian Cross, The Ten Commandments, the American Flag and/or any other traditional American symbols from its location; because someone found it **offensive**.

It is now "**politically correct**" for our Justice Department to *ban* a "photo ID" requirement to vote in our elections even though the process serves as a deterrent to voter fraud… because someone found it **offensive**.

It is now "**politically correct**" for the FBI leadership to *change* counter-terrorism training material which accurately defines a threat to FBI Agents in the field if it makes any *reference* to *Radical Islam* or the word *Terrorism*…because "CAIR" found it **offensive**.

It is now **politically correct** to replace the "Girls" restroom sign with an "All-Gender" restroom sign because of a high-profile "trans-gender" bathroom fiasco. Subsequently, President Obama trivialized the loss of privacy, security and modesty for 99.7 percent of the public in school and public bathrooms, lockers and showers in order to accommodate Transgender students and gender-nonconforming individuals. What part of "indignity" does President Obama not understand? Someone should inform the President that we're not a third-world country…yet.

The lists go on and on as these daily American concessions are being enacted upon to appease the **"Politically Correct Doctrine."** Just recently an organization called "Move On" wants us to drop the letter "I" from *their* newly defined racist-hate word…"Illegal". Apparently, it is now **offensive** to call an illegal immigrant…**illegal.** We are allowing anyone to reverse and mold our country as they see fit and through this unprecedented process we are losing control of our country. It would appear there is a concerted warfare against *Americanism*.

The United State is a country with a conscience that has embraced every nationality, race and religion of the world. But it took the *American rule of law* and an *American culture* to solidify and unify a multi-cultural society devoid of disturbing any person's religion, life style or freedom of choice. *This was the common thread that created a common cause that made America great.* Today, there are those who do not share our American values and are feverously engaged with inciting disunity and chaos within our country in an effort to disable the existence of the *American way of life.* This activity is being accomplished without bullets, but in the name of **"Politically correct."**

This newly resurrected **Politically Correct** Doctrine is a slick anti-American tool masterfully crafted by the

Progressive Left to methodically dismantle our basic freedoms of speech, religion, expression, tradition, etc. which they deem politically incorrect. In other words the architects of **"Politically Correct"** sold us a non-processed declaration stating "Americans need to be more *tolerant*." That false narrative did not complete its concept which is: **Americans need to be more tolerant by relinquishing their American beliefs, their American civil rights and their American Sovereignty unconditionally so as to align with the demands of the intolerant radical left rebels.** *

THE "AMERICAN DREAM" KILLER

By Bunny Herschensohn   **JULY 29, 2012**

Capitalism is "the economic system in which the means of production and distribution are *privately owned and operated for profit*". An alternative to Capitalism is a *Public* economic system whereby the Government defines the means of production and distribution and *owns you* and *your profit*. Today, Capitalism is dying of a progressive disease. On November 6th the American people can decide to cure the disease or stay the course with President Obama's transformation agenda to kill Capitalism.

President Reagan earned the title "The Great Communicator" because his inspirational message to *every* American was a unified, up-lifting, and challenging dialogue which subsequently allowed the "American Dream" to flourish. He also acknowledged the American Dream could only be achieved in a Capitalistic Society in which *The Sky's The Limit* mindset was the norm.

President Obama has earned the title "The Great Divider" because he pits Americans against Americans in an effort to execute a "Divide and conquer" political strategy in his bid for the upcoming election. His relentless attack on the "*rich*" in the name of *fairness*, further demonstrates his contempt for competition. *Competing for excellence* is now being replaced, with a "*leveled playing field*" which only serves to breed *mediocrity* and fuel *envy*. Intimidations, outlandish regulations, and demonizing selective individuals can only restrain dreamers from pursuing their dreams. Add limitations on monetary rewards and you have a government-imposed formula that ultimately kills the "American Dream".

President Obama's progressive agenda has resulted in the instigation and promotion of class warfare, racial hatred, gender inequality, and intolerance towards Christianity, the American rule of law, and "*Americanism*" in any form. Ironically, as these designated groups fight ferociously against each other, President Obama nonchalantly leaves the scene of the crime and moves on to his next prey thus removing himself from any participation or involvement in the chaos and destruction he has created. He is then aided and abetted by our own mainstream American journalists who provide him with convenient escape routes… through their *silence* and *invisibility*.

And so for the first time in American history, we have an "*untouchable*" President who is neither questioned, nor quizzed on his radical politics and is therefore *not* held accountable or responsible for *said* failing policies. Instead, subsequent "*blame games*" and bogus "*racism*" charges have been launched to explain away all the ills of the country. *Sounds like the making of a fine dictator.**

"PERMITS" AND "CODE WORDS"

By Bunny Herschensohn   SEPTEMBER 12, 2012

In Small Town USA, a young child created a *make-shift lemonade stand* in front of her house. Her friends and neighbors praised her initiative but the government did not. She was informed she could not sell her lemonade until she purchased a government *permit*. The cost of the permit was above and beyond any projected profit she could earn selling *lemonade* so this young entrepreneur went out of business.

On a hot blistering summer day in Phoenix, Arizona a Christian group was handing out *free bottles of water* at a festival. A local bureaucrat approached and informed the group they were breaking the law because they didn't have a vender's *permit* labeled "Sidewalk Vending". The Christian group left the festival and the government prevailed in prohibiting a charitable act.

Bunny Herschensohn

A Philadelphia lady was threatened with a $600.00 a day *government fine* for *feeding needy children.* If she wanted to continue this charitable act it would cost her $1000.00. A reporter from "Fox News" offered to pay the $1000.00 fine so she could continue her good work.

These seemingly inconsequential stories reveal unnecessary every day government intrusions into our lives and give us a preview of what Americans can expect in a second Obama term. Not even our words are safe from these ambitious aggressive laws, statutes, regulations and codes. "We The People" are now being accused of using "code words" to mean something more cynical and dangerous than their actual meaning. If you use the word "angry" in the same sentence that includes the words African American…you are a "racist". If you say "hold the fort" you are hostile to American Indians. If you say "illegal" you are expressing hatred toward people of color.

The State Department, the NAACP, the Department of Education, Homeland Security and Politically Correct are now *defining words we cannot say in conjunction with other words.* First our elementary textbooks were doctored. Then our American History books were edited. And now our selective interactive *choice of words* from our dictionaries is being challenged. This subtle

10

words revision transformation alters our "individual thoughts" into a "collective thoughts" ideology.

The Progressives who promote a "leveled playing field" in the name of fairness and equality is yet another false narrative. "Fairness" and "equality" are hardly the words one would use to describe their necessity to decide what every person's income should be. *Control* would be more in keeping. Their passion with an agenda to *control* every man, woman and child in this country, one way or another, is the real narrative. They have expanded and hijacked *our* own legitimate non-intrusive laws to create and establish *their* own coercive dictatorial laws. Subsequently, they are *transforming their heinous system of government control through* our civil system of governance with *words*. We are not becoming Greece; we are becoming subordinates who are surrendering our sovereignty and freedoms without even a murmur. *

UP IS DOWN; RIGHT IS WRONG

By Bunny Herschensohn   OCTOBER 16, 2012

Before President Obama can "fundamentally transform" our American Capitalistic system into a "Socialistic One World Order" he has to first obliterate the *watchdog* and *justification arm* of our Republic...THE FREE PRESS. Over 250 years ago Thomas Jefferson wrote, "Our liberty depends on the Freedom of the press." Hence, the "news media" purportedly is a non-partisan entity that serves to report the news of the day without bias or personal preference or intentional omission and alteration of "said" news. Unfortunately, it appears the "mainstream news media" has collectively dismissed this memo and is now *ignoring* the news instead of *reporting* the news.

The once ethical, respected and fearless "mainstream media" has been reduced to an obedient Obama surrogate. Today, President Obama can tell us, *"Up is down and right is wrong"* without any concern of reprisal through questions of opposition or contradiction from our *impotent* journalists. *Investigative reporting* which brought us the infamous "Watergate" extravaganza appears to be reserved for Republican Administrations only. The once provocative substantive questions asked by robust reporters to all sitting Presidents at White House Press Conferences... are no more. And spontaneous pertinent questions from non-selective reporters at random are but a yesteryear's bygone memory.

Now we are only left with Obama's excessive orchestrated events. Now we have a *"Don't ask, Don't tell"* President of the United States of America emboldened with the power to make crucial decisions that affect every aspect of every American life...*with zero oversight* from the "mainstream media." Thus, the mainstream news media's integrity has been seriously and deliberately compromised and this dangerous precedent can effectively jeopardize our First Amendment's safety net giving Americans the right to criticize their government freely without fear of government intimidation and punishment.

In a Democratic society, there are countless venues and platforms to express *partisan* politics but the "news media" is *not* one of them. Political commentaries, political group discussions, talk shows, the internet, comedic formats, etc., are all outlets for partisans but *reportage*…is *not* one of them. But a funny thing happened on the way to a Presidential election. A mono-on-mono debate took place in which President Obama was actually asked to answer "questions" regarding his past, present and future political policies. He failed that exercise of transparency, decisively. Ironically, because the "mainstream media" *neglected to do their job in 4 years*, a *great imposter was finally exposed to our nation and the world… in one hour.**

THE SMALL PICTURE

By Bunny Herschensohn   **FEBRUARY 12, 2013**

"The Diary of Anne Frank" served as a **reality check** on the persecution of 6 million Jews during World War II. People cannot readily process the obliteration of 6 million people but they are able to relate to **one** person's horrific destiny with strong feelings of sorrow, sadness and compassion which can then transcend to *like* victims with whom they know nothing about. Hence, Hollywood brilliantly personalized the egregious fate of 6 million people by focusing on a story about **one** young girl's documentation of that era. Hollywood understands this human characteristic and filmmakers have used this method, time and time again, to engage the masses that might not otherwise be aware of the injustices and tribulations the multitudes endure within different societies. So why not **personalize your words and visuals of the big picture with an intimate small picture so people can better relate to your total cause.**

"Progressive Democrats" utilize this formula exclusively to validate their agenda successfully. Regrettably, Conservative Republicans do not.

Republicans are relentlessly trying to alert the American people about our *"16 trillion dollar non-stop escalating National debt which will result in America becoming Greece"* with figures, stats and graphs. This is indeed a catastrophic truth but Republicans are not resonating with about 50% of an uninformed apathetic population of the country. These people, oblivious to the consequences that await them, continue to trust this **"cool"** President who, by no coincidence, is the driver on the road of oblivion. Do these Obama supporters even have a clue as to what the end result of this financial nightmare would look like when it collapses? Give a few examples of the changes that will affect their lives profoundly while identifying the cause… **Relentless Government Spending!**

When the government's **borrowing** power is eventually **declined**, the end game will begin. Unfortunately, we will **still** be responsible for trillions of dollars of debt which in turn will **devalue the "dollar"** significantly. I suspect **"cool"** Americans would have a swift change of heart and mindset if suddenly twenty dollars could not even buy a hotdog…if you could find one. Fixed incomes and government welfare would be drastically reduced or terminated**. Obama Care** will incur a shortage of doctors, hidden taxes including taxation of medical devices, 50% higher premiums for young people and **rationing** of all health care as the government sees fit. Costs of our energy essentials such as oil and gas will be "out of sight" and limited. Violent demonstrations could escalate to epic proportions. The lifestyle of the masses would reflect and mirror that of a **Third World** country as Obama's signature **"Fairness"** theme would prevail. Ironically, his **"class warfare"** will **not** affect the rich, the politicians or the elitists. The class warfare doctrine would only serve to **expand poverty** to everyone but those deemed exempt. Their monies and freedoms will remain intact while ours will become a **"shared sacrifice"**. **How fair is this? How cool is this? Get the picture?** *

RACISM, THOUGHTS AND WORDS

By Bunny Herschensohn   APRIL 12, 2013

Webster's dictionary defines **RACISM** as **"the practice of racial discrimination in the belief that some races are inherently superior to others resulting in persecution, etc."** There are no words strong enough to describe this despicable act which plagued our nation for so long. It took many years and many heroes to reverse and evolve from that unconscionable dark place before strong undeniable **progress** began advancing the goal of eradicating racism from our Society once and for all...**until 4 years ago**.

Unfortunately, the Democrat Party including two former Presidents of the United States, Democrat Members of Congress, journalists in the mainstream news media, Union leaders and even the NAACP, have ignored and dismissed this long awaited truism. In addition, they have jointly manufactured a new "racism platform" with an ambitious racial narrative that discredits any Conservative

Bunny Herschensohn

Republican **opposition** to President Obama's political *policies* as *"RACIALLY MOTIVATED"*. Racism has now been deviously recreated and resurrected for personal and political gain by Liberal and Progressive Democrats. I cannot think of anything worse than being called a "**RACIST**" especially when you clearly deplore racism in any form. The ramifications of this accusation are too injurious to overcome as that one word impugns a person's motives, denigrates their integrity, and devalues a person's life *in the blink of an eye*. Still, this malicious and deliberate ploy to crush political opposition through character assassination continues. Our *"fairness"* President, a man of a trillion words, could easily resolve this bigotry with one scolding sentence to his surrogates. But then he would be perceived as "President of *all* the American people." His silence speaks volumes. It is time to end this slanderous attack in the courts. The perpetrators who perpetuate this evil agenda are not justified to **label** persons or organizations **publicly** as **"racially discriminating persecutors."** There should be consequences for this unsubstantiated demoralizing intimidation of predominantly **White Conservative Republicans** or persons of any race or party who *oppose President Obama's political policies*.

Ralph Barker wrote a stunning article called, **"Whoever Controls the Language Controls You"** and references his article to George Orwell's "1984" novel. Sadly, the similarity

22

of this fiction book from *yesteryear* now encapsulates "actuality" in the United States, *today*. This Administration is replacing *Individualism and Freedom* with a dictatorial collective form of government and they are reinforcing this transformation with *"selective words"*. We now have a "Politically Correct" ideological *playbook* that is dictating the words we can and cannot use because we are an *offensive* nation. This agenda is being implemented and justified under the guise that America lacks *Tolerance, Diversity and Inclusion*. Everything we say is being evaluated by **anti-American standards**. But, apparently, **falsely stigmatizing all White Conservatives as "Racists" meets their criteria and is *not* perceived as an offensive action.** So the word **"racist"** is a keeper for the "Word Lords" when applied selectively. But words like Exceptionalism, Patriotism, Illegal Immigrants, Competition, Radical Islamist Terrorists, God, etc., remain on the no-fly list. Our Government is now partaking in the same tactics initiated in the aforementioned prophetic "George Orwell, 1984." Once again, **whoever controls your words controls you.** It's happening right here…right now. Think about this while you can before; **OUR WORDS AND SUBSEQUENT THOUGHTS ARE OUTLAWED.***

SODOM AND GOMORRAH

By Bunny Herschensohn   **SEPTEMBER 1, 2013**

"The Russian people are calling the United States a modern day Biblical Sodom and Gomorrah." Following the G8 Summit, this chilling sentiment was expressed in an article that appeared in the Russian paper, *Pravda*. The story was picked up by an award winning author, Leon Puissegur, who subsequently elaborated on the Pravda piece. In the past, combative Russian remarks regarding the United States have been largely ignored but this disturbing *perception* hit a nerve and got people thinking. Quotes from the *Pravda* article included: *"Christianity triumphs in Russia"* and *"No ACLU in Russia suing Christians to be sure."* It goes on to say; **"The Obama Administration is attacking the Christian core of America. President Obama makes no mention of Christianity under attack in the Middle East and North Africa. Little is mentioned of Christians or Priests murdered in Syria or the Christian Bishops**

that were kidnapped." (End of quotes) As unlikely as the Russian source is, this observation of anti-Christian omission by President Obama is *spot on*. More recently, little is mentioned of the Muslim Brotherhood burning down 50 or more churches during their persecution of Christians in Egypt.

Within the United States there also appears to be a concerted obsession of the Obama Administration and anti-religious groups to disable Christianity by methodically chipping away at Christian symbols, rhetoric and traditions. Could this *war on Christianity* be a factor in the detraining of the morality of our country? "Secular" bias is setting a precedent in which Atheist's demands trump religious freedoms. Are we systematically cultivating a **Sodom and Gomorrah environment** in the United States of America in order to reverse a Judeo/Christian culture? Perhaps, Sharia Law is in our future.

Diversity and **Inclusion** are two words used to fuel a negative atmosphere towards Christianity and our Historical American Foundation. ***"America is not diversified or inclusive enough"*** is the *catch phrase* being spieled by the same people who gave us **"Politically Correct."** And once again, this Administration serves to embrace each and every anti-American project and action that will result in the erosion and elimination of "Americanism" in **any form** from our Society. Our citizenry is the sum total of every religion, every nationality, every race, every gender, and every culture that exists on this planet. **How much more diverse and inclusive can we become?** It appears President Obama wants the United States to become a **multi-cultural** society completely **devoid** of the **American culture**. Ironically, many **American Immigrants fled from** the very cultures President Obama now wants to emulate.

On another note, in March the Senate voted 53-46 (just 4 votes away) to **uphold Second Amendment rights** and prevent the United States from entering into the **United Nations Arms Trade Treaty** which would give our Constitutional rights over to the United Nations.. This *Treaty* championed by the Obama Administration would have affected all private gun owners in the U.S. with the implementation of an international gun registry on all private guns and ammo.

The United States is rapidly losing her Sovereignty and becoming a *nation of the world, by the world and for the world*. Perhaps we will eventually be governed by the United Nations. President Obama is erasing our American Heritage and our American identity while indoctrinating us into oblivion. **Are *American Patriots* about to become the next misplaced refugees of the world?***

WHO ARE THESE PEOPLE?

By Bunny Herschensohn   **DECEMBER 28, 2013**

For the past 5 years the Progressive Liberal Democrats' leadership of Obama's signature **"Fundamental Transformation"** platform has turned our country *"upside down and inside out"* right before our eyes. We now have a government that routinely demonstrates the *irrelevancy of truth* but then adds *300,000* new criminal *regulations* with the force of law to our "Law and Order Doctrine." In a free society, do we really need 300,000 new regulations? Their passionate vision for the "poor", the "sick", the "children" and the "elderly" have now given us a first-hand glimpse into how a Progressive Liberal ideological system of government works. The *poor* have become permanently poor; the *sick* have lost their doctors and hospitals and will be thrown into an inferior dictatorial chaotic system of big government health care; the *children* are being indoctrinated in perpetuity into the collective Progressive Doctrine in order to manifest future Progressive "foot soldiers"; and the *elderly* will be subjected to the *rationing* of everything including *life* itself.

Millionaires have become **multi-millionaires** but the *middle class* has been strategically decimated. We now know that from the beginning it was the *middle class*, not the *rich,* that was targeted to pay for the "**redistribution of wealth**" agenda. From the beginning; it was the *middle class entrepreneurs* and millions of other self-reliant hard working citizens that were the chosen ones to **"Give a little bit more" to correct "income inequalit**y". And from the beginning; the patriotic sacrificial plea was to *reduce* the *middle class standard of living,* in order to equalize compatibility with the low-income sector of our Society. Our symbolic "ladder to success" was replaced with a two-rung ladder with one-rung for the poor and one-rung for the rich. It is now clear the Progressive passionate vision was never *for* the American people at large but for **Bigger Government Power** and **Control** *of* the American people.

The lifestyles of the *rich and famous* were never seriously affected during this transitional period, thus far, because the negative rhetoric *targeting* the *rich* was meant to **dissuade** and **discourage** the *mindset* of those who might strive to pursue their own riches or fame in the future. This is the Progressives' playbook remedy to a **"level playing field"** which fundamentally destroys *individuality,*

competition, creativity and perfection, the very *virtues Capitalism* rewards. Progressives disable an individual's *drive to achieve by accentuating "collective mediocrity."* Many of the Government tax-paid employees that create zero, nothing, nada, appear to occupy that concept. They rule as they see fit through various government agencies and appointed positions without any accountability or reciprocity. Opposing views to any political policies of this Administration is viewed as a threat from *dangerous Americans* and cannot be tolerated. Enter the Progressive **race baiters** whose job is to punish the opposition with one paralyzing stroke of the word, **RACIST.** Let the demonizing begin. Apparently, those who believe in *Capitalism, Freedom of Choice and the American Way of Life* are the enemies of the **Progressive State...This is who these people really are.***

THE STATE OF THE UNION
IN A FEW HEADLINES

By Bunny Herschensohn   **APRIL 10, 2014**

Our national debt is reaching **$18 trillion** and Democrats' response is **"What difference does it make?"**

$6 billion of taxpayer money has been **"misplaced"** by the State Department as accountability of the **lost money** is not possible because there is no paper trail.

President Obama has once again signed the **United Nations "Small Arms Treaty"** which mandates national screenings for all American Citizens seeking to own guns and ammo, restrictions on how many guns and ammo one may own and bans the owning of firearms for self-defense.

Our Space Exploration Program has shut down any future launches and has outsourced our Space technology but has initiated a training program of our Space expertise for

Muslim countries so that "Islamists can feel good about themselves."

The United States has paid Russia **71 million dollars** for **one** of our astronauts to hitch a ride on a Russian Spaceship to the International Space Station…one-way.

President Obama and the Democrats replaced our health care system with Obama Care, 6% of our economy; so that **15 million** uninsured people could have affordable health care only to discover it is the highest tax raise on the middle class in U.S. history, according to the C.B.O. And in the end, **40 million people** will **not** have health care insurance.

Fast and Furious, NSA spying on all Americans citizens, Benghazi and the IRS targeting of Conservatives have all been investigated and concludes no one did anything wrong except in the Benghazi case where justice was done by sending a filmmaker to prison.

There are now **22 million people** working for the Federal Government none of whom have done anything wrong.

EPA and the President oppose every energy strategy to drill and utilize our natural resources but allow Brazil to drill for oil in our part of the Gulf with a promise to that country that we will be their best customer.

In Small Town, USA, a young child who created **a make-shift lemonade stand** in front of her house was told she could not sell her lemonade until she purchased a **government** *permit*, and a 10 year old girl who was making **cupcakes** locally for sale and for charity was told she could not use her Mother's kitchen to make cupcakes but would have to buy a commercial store.

Democrats relentlessly portray Conservatives, Republicans and the Tea Party as **"racists."**

Harry Reid, without any denunciation from fellow Democrats, accuses Conservatives and the Tea Party of being **"Homegrown Terrorists."**

Democrats have stated there is a linkage between **American Veterans** and **"Hate Groups."**

Politically Correct has replaced our Constitution, our Rule of Law, our American way of life and our freedoms because **"World Order"** promulgated by the Progressive Democrats said so.

The United States is no longer a **Judeo-Christian nation** and any reference to **God**, as in the Pledge of Allegiance, has been found to be offensive to the Atheists.

These are just a few of the beautiful things.*

A CIVICS MEMO TO COLLEGE GRADUATES

By Bunny Herschensohn **MAY 3, 2014**

We've all heard the humorous phrase **"Old age is not for sissies"** but these days it appears **"Self-reliance is also not for sissies."** Regrettably, we are seeing an uncharacteristic rise in the number of people seeking out "entitlement programs" as if they were applying for a job. Arguably, the work drop-out stats may be as a result of today's anemic economy that is *not* providing a robust job market but whatever the cause, it is *not* good news. Fortunately, our government provides us with a "safety net" (tax-payers money) to help those individuals who have fallen into bad times. Many gratefully use it but many misguided individuals abuse it. Keep in mind our political system only thrives when tax payers do.

"**Charity**" is also promoted and encouraged as a good and selfless act that everyone should want to adopt accordingly. Americans have the reputation of being the most charitable people in the world because of their individual decision to consistently give of their time and/or money to the cause of their choice. And, in spite of a few greedy bad eggs in the mix, Americans give from their heart and they give willingly. **That's our American Culture.**

Success, by all accounts, can only be defined objectively through the eyes of the beholder whose dreams, needs, and wants are as diversified as *they* are. However, personal success can only be achieved and accomplished in an environment in which one has the infinite freedom to *pursue* their choices without interference from an over-bearing government. Unlike many countries of the world, our **Capitalistic Free Market System** of Governing offers the **greatest process** to accomplish these sometimes difficult but rewarding challenges. Although, some Americans are discarding this gift of opportunity; for many it is a motivating factor that compels millions of people from around the globe to immigrate to "America" legally and illegally.

Structurally, the RICH, the MIDDLE CLASS and the POOR are so named and loosely categorized into a three bracket Capitalistic economic system of measurement for the purpose of identifying an individual's financial status… at the time. However, because these calculations are only relative to another's income, in no way is this classification a *permanent financial station.* The **Middle Class** sector, serves as **"the little engine that could"** and keeps the whole system running as the **Middle Class** is not only a **step up** from the poor but becomes a **stepping stone** to the rich bracket. Under our system, this ever moving criterion provides your individual ambitions with a **"no limits barred"** provision and is all in your hands. This is how and why **Capitalism** works and this is also why *there will always be income inequality.* Therefore, our Government cannot equalize or guarantee any person's income in the market place through Federal Law. To do so, **everyone's employer** would have to **be the Government.** That system has always been in existence in one Socialistic fashion or another worldwide and is what distinguishes **"Americans"** from millions of people living in stagnate poverty or even bondage and servitude.

Why would you make a trade off from *Liberty, choice* and *opportunity* to sameness, stagnation and a predetermined outcome on all things? **Income equality** sounds admirable at face value but never results in a righteous outcome. For many compassionate proponents who are sincere in their outreach to help people, income equality/socialism is not the solution. For many leaders who promote it; **power over the people** is their prime motivation and socialism is the vehicle that delivers the means. For others; *envy* is the warped mindset which we know is never satisfied…. So let's call it what it is…a deceitful flawed concept.

The *Progressive Liberal Democrats,* the majority of college Professors and a host of other renowned supporters right from the book of "Who's Who" are promoting a political ideology that locks you into a *"one size fits all" income outcome* for life, in the bogus quest for "fairness." And since income determines your lifestyle, we have to wonder if the Obamas, the Clintons, George Clooney, Jay Z, Bill Gates, Oprah, Susan Sarandon, Barbra Streisand, etc. would be willing to live the same lifestyle they are advocating for all of us. I think not. They keep their riches and we get fairness.

The Progressive's solution of **income equality** for everyone is a façade and a crock because there will always be a selected privileged group of people including *"They Who Rule"* who will always be above the pay grade of an income equality proclamation. Do the Russian people live as well as Putin does? As Government grows, so do government regulations until *freedoms of choice are nowhere to be found.* In America's Capitalistic free trade system, you can *work* for the government or you can *work* for private enterprise or you can open up a candy store and *work for yourself.* The common denominator for all three of these choices is you can quit. The choice is unlimited and the decision is all yours. **That's the beauty of the American Free Enterprise System at work and at its best.**

If we continue to embrace this anti-American doctrine, promulgated by the liberal extremists, your decision-making days will be in the hands of everyone...but yours. **America's Dreamers, America's Free Spirit and America's Sovereignty will be no more and you will be of no consequence... with or without a college diploma.***

SELF-DESTRUCTION

BY Bunny Herschensohn   **MAY 26, 2014**

World opinion tells us the United States of America is no longer *respected* or *feared* but looks more like a nation that is on a self-destructive course to decline. "Self-destruction" is one of the most challenging tendencies to overcome in life. And although "self-destruction" by its very name indicates *singular* bad behavior, it can also manifest into a *collective* body of bad behavior given a contagion type of environment. Unfortunately, the Progressive Liberal Democrats have created and provided such an environment that feeds off this ill-fated trend of bad behavior, nationwide. America's work ethic of self-reliance and self-esteem has been reversed to government dependency and redistribution of wealth. A Socialistic agenda, contrary to our American values, is not only an embodiment and pre-curser to a *dictatorial government controlled society*, but is also an aggressive contributing factor that progressively promotes self-destruction both individually and collectively.

In the process to solidify Socialism, the Progressives in the United States have declared "War" on the American people and every American Institution that does not reflect, relate or correspond to their manifesto. But, unlike traditional wars; this one is being waged by orchestrated words of deceit. "Politically Correct" are the guns and bombs of this war. "Politically Correct" is identity theft of our American Culture and our American Sovereignty. "Politically Correct" dictates concessions commensurate with that made by a defeated country that has lost a war, surrendered and is obligated to acknowledge the mandated terms. One of those terms includes the loss of individual *Freedom of Speech, thought, ideas* and *expression* that do not corroborate Progressive standards. Added to this package is an intimidating disobedience clause, punishable by the MOB SQUAD. *Individualism* and *Competition* is to Progressives what sunshine and daylight is to vampires and is an unacceptable practice. "Politically Correct" is now America's self-destructive Rule of Law.

On this Memorial Day, as we watch the National Memorial Day Parade on Constitution Avenue in Washington, DC, we are reminded of how unique and precious our history was sustained by so many brave and selfless American men and women who made the ultimate sacrifices to ensure our freedoms for the past 200+ years. Since our inception we have faced many adversarial challenges from the American Revolution forward and all were fought on behalf of a human right and desire to be free none as determined or evident as our own devastating Civil War. Today, we are faced with an internal political party that threatens our hard fought freedoms for a "pseudo-pie in the sky" ideology that has failed miserably in every country it was implemented. The short term goal of the Progressives is total government power over a helpless, fearful and freedom-less "We the People." The long term goal is *World Global* domination of America whereby there will be no difference economically and spiritually between America and all the other third-world countries around the world.

If we lose this battle, "they rule and we obey." That will be our legacy to a futuristic America. Is this *why* Americans throughout our history worked so hard and died so heroically to preserve our freedoms? I don't think so.*

AMERICA

By Bunny Herschensohn   **11/09/2014**

As we assess the 2014 midterm election results, all evaluations of this devastating loss for the Democrats should come into play. In the words of President Obama, "Elections have Consequences." Hence, this election should be no different. The general consensus states the *"Stagnate Economy"* as the number one reason the Democrats suffered such a defeat as all indicators confirm the decimation of the *middle class*. People are *not* better off today than they were 6 years ago. But, there are other reasons as well.

The Democrat Party is no longer the liberal party of yesteryear. Today it is the Progressive Party selling an ideology that is contrary to everything America stands for. It is an entity within itself that is purely self-serving. In the past, our historical political protocol indicates that both political parties have always "agreed to disagree" without any ramifications from either side; but this new Progressive

Democrat party does not adhere to this precedent. Individuals who oppose Progressive policies are personally demonized and punished with intimidating consequences from various government agencies such as the IRS, EPA and the Justice Department. The Progressive Democrat Party's playbook has become more sinister in their quest to defeat Republican candidates. The new goal appears to advocate complete *unilateral control* of America and the American people devoid of any competition or contradiction from Congress, the Republican Party and the 2-party system.

When the DNC Chair says Republicans are *scarier than ISIS and EBOLA*…something is wrong. When Harry Reid, without any denunciation from fellow Democrats, accuses Conservatives and the Tea Party of being "*HOMEGROWN TERRORISTS*"…something is wrong. When Democrats have stated there is a linkage between American Veterans and *HATE GROUPS*…something is wrong. And when Democrats relentlessly portray Republicans, Conservatives and the Tea Party as "*RACISTS*", this pathetic attempt of vilification defies all historical facts recorded as the following would suggest. It was a Republican President who ended slavery in the United States. The SUPPORT RESULTS of the 13th, 14th and 15th Amendments are as follows:

13th Amendment:	**ABOLISHED SLAVERY**	100% REPUBLICAN
		23% DEMOCRAT
14th Amendment:	**GAVE CITIZENSHIP to**	94% REPUBLICAN
	FREED SLAVES	0% DEMOCRAT
15th Amendment:	**RIGHT to VOTE FOR ALL**	100% REPUBLICAN
		0% DEMOCRAT

The chief support for the Civil Rights Bill of 1964 was from Senator Everett Dirksen (Republican) and a coalition of Republicans and Democrats. President Lyndon B. Johnson (Democrat) signed the Bill even though as a United States Senator, he voted *against every Civil Rights Bill.* Only *64 percent* of Democrats in Congress voted for the 1964 Civil Rights Act while *80 percent* of Republicans voted for the 1964 Act. Robert C. Byrd, the revered Democrat Senator, 1959-2010, served as a recruiter and leader of the Ku Klux Klan *(a club exclusively comprised of democrats)* and as recently as 2005 in his memoir, Byrd describes the KKK as a fraternal assembly of "upstanding people." Really?

Under Democrat governing, the American people have been doled a daily barrage of *Ridicule*, where ridicule was not warranted, *Division*, where unity was prevailing and *Confusion* and *Chaos* where stability was the norm. Common sense was replaced with ambiguous rhetoric and disorganization. In their quest to *reinvent America,* we were emphatically informed *"You didn't build that"*, *"Americans are not exceptional"* and *"We are not a Judea-Christian nation."* They have rebuked and rebutted every American Institution and every trickle of American Culture we painstakingly built by implementing their leftist ideology with hostile laws, thousands of regulations, propaganda and indoctrination that view us as an evil empire that has to be destroyed.

President Obama and the Progressive Democrats, as well as many enemies around the world, do not like America. But, **Americans love America***. They woke up, voted and in a loud voice said,* **"No mas! No more!"** *

JUST SAY NO

By Bunny Herschensohn **APRIL 20, 2015**

Today, we are facing two enemies simultaneously. Both are fueled with hatred and disdain towards America. One of these serious adversaries is the ***Radical Islamic Extremists*** who shield their faces but not their medieval barbarism. These sub-human degenerates who call themselves **ISIS, AL QAEDA, BOKO HARAM**, or whatever, are constantly evolving and merging with other Islamic cells who share their religious fanaticism world-wide. Of course, the granddaddy of them all is ***IRAN***, a state sponsor and chief exporter of terrorism in the region whose goal is to obtain nuclear weapons, and to extend their *expansion mode*, at will. Although names may vary, their collective brutality is consistent and compatible with their mutual *objective* which is ***Sharia Law for everyone and death for everyone else.*** *To date there is no official coherent U.S. strategy available, regarding this matter.*

The second foe is *"The Democratic Socialists of America"* **(DSA).** *Socialism* has always been a bit player on our political stage but was never a threat to our Constitution, our liberties or our American way of life. However, that scenario changed drastically the day President Obama announced he was going to *" fundamentally transform"* our country. Unfortunately, most Americans who are not skeptics by nature were totally oblivious to the derogatory *intent* and *harm* this *ambiguous* Declaration would impose on our political system since the Obama Administration would *shun clarity* when initiating their undefined agenda. Today it is crystal clear that *all* their devious transformations are intentionally presented and executed under an *umbrella of ambiguity.* Unlike the Islamic terrorists who flaunt their narrative both verbally and visually; the Socialists, aka Secular Progressives aka Liberal-Left Democrats, are *not* transparent. They deliberately and methodically camouflage their agenda to discredit and destroy our Constitutional system of governing under the pretext of implementing social justice for everyone. In the real world, this ideology, a redistribution of wealth, was structured exclusively *by* big government, *for* big government and negates the *will of the people.* President Reagan said it best; *"The nine most terrifying words from the English language are, I'm from the government and I'm here to help."* Under this Democrat Administration, **Free Market Capitalism is on its way out and Big Government Socialism is the wave of our future.**

The Democrat Party, who once took pride in the creation of a political system that promoted and screamed *Individual Freedoms for all*; has now succumbed to an inexplicable **anti-American totalitarianism regime**. This drastic reversal from freedom of choice to a notion that *people are incapable of making choices,* has given credence to *Big-Government Rule, as well as Kingdoms and Dictatorships.* And the one common trait that embodies all these ideologues is a fanciful belief of *individual superiority over others* and of course; the unlimited personal gain of money and power afforded only to them. They traded our American foundation for *"The End Justifies the Means"* anthem of the left-wing extremists. They then went on to sell their anti-American ideology with slick talking points comprised of an *either/or policy* of intimidation to nearly half of the country through deceit, bribes, racism and propaganda. Examples of their two-choice options go something like this; "Either we adopt Obama Care or millions of people will die." "Either we accept the Iran Nuclear Deal or we go to War." It's either their way or Armageddon. Now make your choice.

War is in the wind all right but it is the Socialist Democrats who have declared War on anything and everything that speaks…America. And even though this confrontation does not mirror previous wars where heavy artillery and loss of life was the means in which the battles were fought; it is still a war in which **"Winner Takes All"** is afforded to the victor just as it would in a traditional war... And in this case the enemy's *prize* is the dissimulation of America.

Through carefully selected *ATTACK WORDS* the Liberal-left accuses and indicts our country of fictitious wrongdoing, relentlessly. Therefore, it is important for people to recognize how they use fair-minded words disingenuously in order to persuade. They would have us believe we lack MULTI-CULTURISM, DIVERSITY, TOLERANCE and INCLUSIVENESS within our political system. This is not only very perplexing but dishonest since the very essence of America's fundamental concept was MULTI-CULTURISM, DIVERSITY, TOLERANCE and INCLUSIVENESS from its inception. These are the substantive components that have always defined us. Therefore, 239 years later as America continues to evolve into a more perfect Union because of this successful formula, the opposition's whole narrative is a lie. The Liberal Left's bogus incriminations against America were purposely initiated to create racial-unrest, distrust, division, and discontent within our population. The goal is to re-create *America's Culture* into a *United Nations culture* in order to diminish and eventually terminate our **American** Patriotism, our **American** Rule of Law, and our **American** Sovereignty. Another word they love to beat their drums with is "**OFFENSIVE**." Through their newly adopted "POLITICALLY CORRECT RULES" the operative word "offensive" gives one single individual or a handful of people the power to override our "MAJORITY RULES" and can in turn be used to deny an American citizen of their freedoms, values or traditions. A display of the AMERICAN FLAG, THE TEN COMMANDMENTS, CHRISTMAS, etc., have all been put on the chopping block in the name of "OFFENSIVE."

To quote President Obama, ***"elections have consequences."*** So for starters; Vote every Democrat *out of office* and vote "NO" to any future Democrat candidates; until they get their act together. Remember, their vote trumps your vote to live in a free Society. The Socialists are well aware that unilateral control of a people; necessitates unilateral control of an election's outcome. And although they were successful in converting many citizens to abandon their proud allegiance to the American way of life, others rejected the transformation. There were those who would not be manipulated or coerced into changing their pro-American and Judea/Christian beliefs as a whole and who still stand in their way to this day. Therefore, change and revision of an uncooperative patriotic element is necessary for the hard-left ideology to take hold permanently. One such counteraction to that component is an unlimited **importation** of preconditioned immigrants through our open borders. This newly enacted policy enables the Left ideologists with an alternate solution to the problem in hand.

Five million new illegal immigrants including children who have crossed our borders recently was neither a coincidence nor a spontaneous move but a coordinated effort on the part of the Democrat Party to garner votes in future elections by eventually changing the **demographics** of the United States. As an incentive, President Obama continues to give a shout-out to Central America by assuring them they will be immune to Deportation. Word is out the **State Department** is even flying illegal immigrants from their perspective countries to the good old U.S.A. And of course, all are encouraged to get drivers licenses which include Party Registration and a food stamp box. Isn't it ironic that *no cost* is too great to **import millions of illegals**; while in the past, *high cost* was the explanation given for *not securing the border* or *implementing Deportation*? **Five million unidentified people** have crossed our borders and a second batch is on its way. Meanwhile American citizens are being barraged with thousands of new government laws, regulations, permits, codes and taxes that are stripping us of our God-given freedoms and are instrumental in the dismantling of our country; on a daily basis. This is a hard pill to swallow. **America is being Invaded by the world *not* for Humanitarian reasons but to protect and preserve the building of a more secure Socialist Secular State; compliments of the Democrat Party and their henchmen; the pathetic mainstream monolithic Liberal News Media.**

If we lose this war, there can be no compromise and no turning back as we will become powerless and inconsequential. Eventually we will just be another impoverished nation devoid of Civil Liberties.

So now with the realization that the Democrat Party has been compromised by a **hostile** manifesto that **uses** our system to **destroy** our system; it is incumbent upon Patriotic Legislators and Patriotic Citizens to stop the Democrats from accomplishing their goal of *fundamentally transforming America* from a "Shining City on the Hill" to a slimy city in rubble.

Just say, "NO" to all Democrats running for office in the upcoming Presidential election.

GOD SHOWED UP BRIEFLY

By Bunny Herschensohn   JULY 10, 2015

"Actions Speak Louder than Words" is a phrase often heard that most folks would agree is sound advice. But, as aphorisms go, there are always counter contradictory adages as well; *"The Pen is Mightier than the Sword"* is just such an example. One can only conclude both aphorisms are equally true and equally powerful depending on how and when they are used. President Obama and his Administration tend to misuse these truisms on a regular basis. Case in point; A President cannot draw a red line and **leave it at that** especially when the red line is crossed. That situation demands *action*, not words. On the other hand, a President cannot disclose racial epithets that incite rage which then emboldens others to partake in unlawful actions and **leave it at that**. In this case, his omission of words becomes **passive actions** that inflame and subsequently trigger a *racial divide* throughout the country. Hence, words can create as much havoc as

actions, given certain circumstances. Not exactly a steadfast formula for the unification of a nation.

In total contrast, we all heard *3 little words* that were nothing less than *stunning* uttered by a broken-hearted group of family members who had just suffered a cold blooded racist massacre of their loved ones. **"I FORGIVE YOU"** were the words that literally unified a battered and sickened nation. **"I FORGIVE YOU"** were the 3 golden words the good families told the evil perpetrator face to face at a Bond hearing. Although most of us could not fathom this charitable response under such horrific circumstances, these extraordinary Christian Americans amidst such a tragedy "walked the walk" to show us all how **Good** can win over **Evil.** And for a brief moment, as we watched thousands of people Black and White *united* hand and hand walk across a bridge together, we were reminded of America's exceptionalism. In this case, the Pen was mightier than the Sword.

But, alas that God-like defining moment would be short-lived as the Liberal Left Media and the Progressive Democrats would have none of that. The talking points were swiftly switched to the Confederate Flag and gun control. After all, "control" not harmony, is what the Liberal Socialists do best. Although removing the Confederate Flag from the South Carolina State House was a good thing, that action has escalated to the banning of anything and everything remotely associated with the Southern Confederacy of the past. Once again, the Democrats' motto, "Never let a good crises go to waste" prevails and once again America's History is being altered. Never mind the Historical value of the statues, monuments and landmarks. Just destroy and erase. Rename the schools, roads and towns, ban "The Dukes of Hazards" and exhume bodies from their graves. And that's just the beginning of what's to come.

The History of any country, good, bad or indifferent simply records and verifies its mere existence. And since America has such a short history it is important this time-table of events is preserved as a gauge to show how we self-correct injustice and unjust practices in a true Democracy. It shows the world how a *good* country strives to evolve to a more perfect Union. And it shows how a mindset can grow and change for the better in a free society. You don't delete the data of a Civilized Nation's journey because it wasn't pretty. But evidently, the Progressive Democrats want to do just that. However, in defense of the Democrats who now incessantly and falsely use the race card against Republicans 24/7, they probably feel compelled to destroy all historical evidence surrounding racism and slavery since it clearly indicts the Democrats; not the Republicans.

The Confederates and the Ku Klux Clan were all Democrats and it was the Democrats who imposed "Jim Crow" laws. It was the Democrats who voted *against* the 13th Amendment

(Abolished Slavery) the 14th Amendment (Gave Citizenship to Freed Slaves) and the 15th Amendment (Right to Vote for All). And while only 64% of the Democrat law makers voted for the 1964 Civil Rights Act; no Democrat voted to ostracize their most revered Democrat Senator Robert Byrd. He was a recruiter and leader of the Ku Klux Klan, who as recently as 2005 in his memoir described the KKK as a fraternal assembly of "upstanding people."

No, it's not our History that should be erased; it's today's hypocritical race-baiter's rhetoric that should be erased from the face of the earth.*

THE REDISTRIBUTION OF FREEDOM

By Bunny Herschensohn   **DECEMBER 25, 2015**

"Every step we take towards making the State our Caretaker of our lives, by that much we move toward making the State our Master."
Dwight D. Eisenhower

To this end, *all* of President Obama's calculated steps have moved us closer towards making the *"State our Master."* His progressive core values and anti-American sentiments have finally taken its toll on a nation that was once civil and objective to a divisive country that is now in total disarray and unrecognizable. President Obama may not be interested in a military strategy to defeat *"ISIS"* but he most certainly has mastered a strategy to defeat *America's Constitutional Principles, America's Rule of Law and* America's *Ideology.*

Of special interest to President Obama is his *selective* intervention into social issues such as religion, abortion and sexual preferences. His aggressive emphasis on gay marriages and transgenderism has been nothing short of confrontational and divisive. The American people, in general, have no interest at all in condemning or applauding another person's sexual preference. Yet, today they are now *mandated* to become a *participant* at the expense of relinquishing their own civil liberties. Millions of people are being forced to make life changing adjustments to accommodate the sexual preferences of a few. There are 37,000 pages of changes regarding passports and Birth Certificates that are being altered to read "Parent 1 and Parent 2" in place of "Mother and Father." In other areas, school children are not to be distinguished or addressed as "boys and girls" and gender neutrality now dictates the dismissal of gender privacy in school bathrooms and locker rooms. *"Neuter the genders"* appears to be one of this Administration's pet projects as majorities are now forced to obey and accommodate that which the *minority* demands without *due process of law or sensibility*. Whereas, every political and social component of America's culture was so created and structured to give each and every individual the personal freedom of choice, that premise is no longer viable. One person's freedom of choice is now *valued* more than another's freedom of choice. This biased substitution and designated replacement of freedoms can only be construed as the *redistribution of all our freedoms*.

Because of his "one size fits all" Obama Care creation, 80 Catholic Hospitals are under attack for not providing *abortions*. Also, included in this debacle are "The Little Sisters of the Poor" who are *religiously bound* against all or any form of birth control participation and were subsequently sued by this Administration. Ironically, this same Administration represented a case in which two Muslim truckers were fired for refusing to make deliveries of beer for their employers because of *their* religious beliefs. The Muslims won the case by a jury presided over by an Obama appointee and were awarded $240,000. Not so lucky were the Christian owners of "Melissa's Sweet Cakes" who were fined $135,000 for refusing to bake a wedding cake for a lesbian couple because of their religious beliefs. In the mid-east, Christians are being tortured and killed mercilessly while in the United States, Christianity is perpetually being targeted with attacks on its beliefs, symbols and traditions in one way or another including those who are hell bent on silencing and eliminating the harmless celebrated phrase..."Merry Christmas!" In Obama's America, religious freedoms apply to some but not all which further demonstrates and encapsulates his *"redistribution of our freedoms"* policy.

In order to disrupt and corrupt America's way of life, President Obama had to challenge our young people's mindset by removing all pre-existing conceptions. Faith, family, American History, self-reliance and respect for law and order, to name a few, had to be discarded.

Regarding Faith; when our Judeo-Christian guidelines to civility such as the *Ten Commandments or even something as mundane as prayer, etc.* are minimized, mocked and muted, "right and wrong" becomes ambiguous and non-distinguishable. The omission of *Spirituality* creates a big *vacuum* in a person's psyche. And that void can have a very confusing and destructive effect on young people whose inexperienced thought process is vulnerable and in play.

This is especially problematic since there is a serious Progressive filtered indoctrination agenda going on in our elementary schools and universities throughout the nation. The objective is to marginalize, reject and trade our core values, Capitalism and a free Sovereignty for an International Collective Socialistic alternative. In order to apply *change*, this movement must first reverse the norm. For starters, children are now treated as adults and adults as children. A twelve-year old child has access to birth control contraceptives in school *without* a parent's *consent* while a twenty-six year old child can stay on his parent's health insurance policy. Unbeknownst to these misguided children/adults, who lack self-discipline, strength and purpose; when an individual's life is devoid of any past history, faith and foundation… *direction is not feasible; however manipulation is inevitable.*

This just might explain the *"Me, My Selfie and I"* generation who appear to have a higher concentration and exaggerative emphasis on one's "feelings" than anything else. Some even find solace in becoming a *victim*. Today, it is now noble and fashionable to *be* an *offended victim* especially since *Politically Correct* has their back. Hence, if you are not a real victim; create and use a situation in which you can be one. The obstructive "Politically Correct" pseudonym and a person's mumbo-jumbo "feelings" appear to go hand and hand. The idea that systematically one person's sensitivity can now justify the theft of another person's freedom is again a redistribution of freedoms and a non-compliance of every American's Constitutional Rights. It appears the *real clouded goal of young people is to become "relevant"…anyway they can.*

President Obama's vision of molding our mindset permanently to his liking is now being channeled *through the mouths of babes* and is progressing very well. So through this young captive audience his *"Fundamentally Transformation"* doctrine will continue. And with the indoctrination tools of PC (*politically correct*) and CC (*climate change*) our next generation of Americans will be remembered as DDD (*Dumb, Dependent Democrats.*) *

SUMMARY

REINVENTING AMERICA…THE LAST STRAW!

By Bunny Herschensohn   SEPTEMBER 10, 2017

America is more divided than anyone ever imagined and President Donald Trump is a result, *not the cause of such a polarized country.* The division and polarization in total is a working product of a *leftist radical liberal movement* that hit the jackpot when they finally became *relevant* in the Obama Administration. But, when the baton was *not* passed to Hillary Clinton, the Democrat's aggressive agenda of *"reinventing America"* was abruptly halted. So after a tumultuous and unprecedented Presidential election and against all odds, *Middle America* won the battle to preserve *America's Sanctity and Sovereignty…* *so they thought.*

Regrettably, even in the wake of this major upset, it pales in comparison to the unthinkable but *successful anti-American revolutionary culture* the Progressive Democrats have engineered through skillful recruitment and indoctrination agendas for the past several years. Hence, today two disjointed contrary ideological views *of and for* America have manifested into the catastrophic state of affairs we are now witnessing. The following analysis is how some of this may have been contrived and coordinated into the reality it is today.

The defeated *players* consisting of countless long-term politicians, pundits and operatives with a heavily vested interest in this Presidential election lost their lethal leftist stronghold on the country overnight. This also touched President Obama who routinely reiterated *his legacy was on the ballot.* Specific groups caught in this tangled web of repudiation included the Progressive Democrat Party and the Socialists, Academia and the Anarchists, liberal pollsters and lobbyists, a massive and imposing liberal bureaucracy, wealthy notable liberal surrogates from the entertainment industry and of course the non-objective Mainstream News Media whose *collusion* with the Democrat Party did not end well for them this time around.

For all these people; President Trump is an absolute nightmare primarily because *he is not one of them* especially since by all accounts he *should* be one of them. That in itself is an exasperating and revolting dilemma for the Democrats. As to the professional politicians, Trump is a non-ideologue *outsider* who has won his way into the *insider's turf,* a private domain for long-standing members only. So because he is not beholden to anyone, he poses a threat to *everyone* including many Republicans who opposed him from the outset.

But in lieu of such a stormy environment that prevails today, all Republicans should now evaluate a different scenario for a moment. Even if a more traditional mainstream Republican candidate had won this Presidential election; the ferocious hostility and obscene lack of civility that permeates our country today would still have come to pass as this election was not about traditional politicians or traditional issues. This was a serious minded election that interrupted a serious left-wing undertaking that was shredding our Constitution, and stripping us of our individuality to *Freedom of Speech.* The agenda was replacing and revising our American History, our American Rule of Law, our Judeo-Christian core values and our political landscape by altering the composition of our citizenry.

These American *architects of anarchists* were reinventing "America" through a lens that abhors and resents *said* country in its totality. Therefore no Republican candidate would have ever been acceptable to the *anarchists* at this time unless they were on board with the above stated deranged Progressive playbook. But as fate would have it, Donald Trump was victorious and like him or not; he is now the *only* person in the world today who can *save our legacy, our liberty and our lives from a destiny of demise*. Regrettably, without substantial support not yet received…it is not a given.

To date, the losers still have no plans for serious introspection but have instead focused only on removing President Trump from office. They portray him as the biggest monster the world has ever seen as they dissect and impugn every word he utters. They have collectively attacked his family, his staff and his Cabinet selections viciously with personal ridicule and have labelled all those who voted for him (over 63million strong) "*dumb and deplorable racists*".

These radicals have collectively vowed to resist and reject this President's entire agenda by *blocking everything* including *freedom of speech…24/7*. With these people, nothing is sacred or over the top as there are no limits in this savage liberal contest to crucify Donald Trump and his constituents. *Vulgarity* and *abusive mobs* of demonstrators rule the day and have now replaced the dignity and respect of a civilized society. Nothing will please them short of impeachment or death of the duly elected President of the United States of America.

All of these unmasked reactions further unveil why the Democrats lost in the first place as it spotlights and reveals their true aspirations and ruthlessness in real time and confirms how important this election really was. As to the victors; they experienced a *momentary sigh of relief* amidst a never ending dangerous atmosphere of disruptive and intimidating rage aimed directly against them. Individually, all of these actions border on insanity the likes of which we have never seen before. Collectively, they are undermining America's election results by obstructing and sabotaging America's governing process at every turn. If this is not *anarchy or a coup heading towards Armageddon ...then what is?*

"Ask not what your country can do for you but what you can do for your country." ...President John F. Kennedy

That was then. This is now. Today, many Americans (approximately 47%) hold a position that *Government*, not the individual, has the responsibility to financially support them from cradle to grave. Once again, this nanny state ideology was harvested and achieved through the former Socialistic-driven Administration whose primary goal was not to benefit the American people but was designed to obtain absolute power exclusively for the *new Progressive Democrat Party.*

Keep in mind, the new Progressive Democrat Party is *not* the same Democrat Party your parents and grand-parents revered and trusted in the past. That Party no longer exists and has been hijacked into oblivion. Today's Democrat Party is now the *Party of Hatred* and is likened to a Socialist or Communist-run party in which all objectives, emphasis and rationale *is on behalf of the Party, not the People.* Frozen and lost in this political transformation was America's sacred creed whereby *self-reliance ensures liberty* while *government controlled societies evolve into bondage.* The sharp contrast between these two political ideologies is as stark as the *burqa is to the bikini and* is precisely why Congress was so dysfunctional the previous 8 years as there can be no common ground between the two conflicting incompatible ideologies. *Collectivist Socialism works for government and dictatorships... Capitalism AND THE FREE MARKET works for the People.*

"You didn't build that"...President Barack Obama

The majority of Americans, with the exception of a small fringe group of despicable bigots, enthusiastically embraced and celebrated our landmark election of the first African American President with the sincere belief he would serve America and *all the American people well*. For others who reserved their endorsement of the new President, they did so because they were at odds with his Progressive political ideology; *not the color of his skin*. On that significant political note, only time and the new President's actions would confirm or disprove the skeptic's sincere and legitimate concerns.

However, right out of the gate President Obama responded loud and clear. The skeptic's concerns of the President-Elect's left-leaning ideology was realistically confirmed with his harsh policies that gave us an unprecedented agenda of obsessive rules, permits, statutes, taxation, obstructive regulations and the inevitable Obamacare, a preamble to *single payer* health care.

What was *neither expected nor anticipated* was his *undoing* of what most Americans worked so hard to repair over the decades regarding *race relations*. Prior to Obama's Presidency, *racial unity* was slowly but surely progressing favorably towards building a *just* and *righteous* drum beat for all... a happening never before witnessed. Unfortunately, Barack Obama would have none of this and simply ignored all previous positive *advances* that actually embraced racial solidarity. Instead there was a shift in attitude to not only re-visit the past of racial strife but *to re-create and re-establish a revamped racially divided country...once again.*

And with his "You didn't build that" commentary that scorned personal achievements, he appeared to hold an unprecedented disdain for *individualism, self-reliance, and competition*; three components of Capitalism that made America Great. Soon it became abundantly clear President Obama and his Administration were not serving America well but were following a new course to *reinvent America* which would in no way mirror the successful formulated fabric the Founding Fathers envisioned and created.

"Hating a Person's Color Is Wrong and It Doesn't Matter Which Color Does the Hating" ...Muhammad Ali (1942-2016)

As stated earlier, even though an overwhelming majority of the American people did *not* find Barack Obama's skin color to be of any consequence or significance, the new President-elect along with his Progressive Democrats held a more cynical self-serving view in believing otherwise. Evidently, their leftist agenda necessitated a fast knock-out punch distraction more potent than a bomb in their *narrative arsenal* in order to excoriate any opposition they would face while implementing their *radical political transformation*. That distraction would be to engage in one of the most diabolical and paralyzing words in our vocabulary ...*racist.*

This one vile word has the capacity and unwarranted power to dehumanize, discredit and vanquish a person or groups of persons in the blink of the eye, without any justification or legal procedure. For the guilty… the punishment fit the crime. But for the *falsely accused* … the punishment was a travesty of justice. And so it was. Any opposition of Obama's political policies was construed as an attack on his race. Hence, our sacred creed of *"Innocent until Proven Guilty" became "Guilty by Accusation."*

"A Lie Told Often Enough Becomes the Truth"…Vladmir Lenin

Our First Amendment's safety net giving Americans the right to criticize their government freely without fear of government intimidation and punishment became a non-existent entity during the Obama Administration. And it would not be long before just the *threat* of being labeled a "racist" stifled freedom of speech and silenced much of the opposition on all political and social issues. In short, President Obama became our first *untouchable President because of his race.*

Emboldened by the success of this branding by shaming formula; a whole gambit of other character *assassination words* such as *Sexist, Homophobes, Xenophobes, Islamophobias, etc.* were all assimilated into a grand degradation program of *deceptive identity politics.* The accused virtually had no shot at all against back-up *armies of angry mobs and bullies who* were then assembled into massive orchestrated *demonstrations to serve as Judge and Jury.* Innocent people's reputations and livelihoods were destroyed publicly as these massive gang-ups coming from all directions were covered relentlessly by the press and social media.

Today, that *false racist* subjectivity is interjected into all matters of consequence as a valid talking point. *Every issue now has a negative racial component.* And in the process of such an ambitious and repetitive narrative that relentlessly defines all white people as *racists;* an inflammatory and irrefutable discrimination towards an *entire race* was created. It is now politically correct and the norm to *accuse* all white people of being *"Privileged White Racists"* and *"White Supremacists."* This unfounded *nation-wide generalization and condemnation* of a specific race or religion is reminiscent of Hitler's actions during the 1930's when he enacted a nationalized "hate campaign" against all Jews.

Truth be told; we do have a privileged class within our society called "CELEBRITIES" who are coincidentally diversified in every sense of the word as they come in *all colors* and are from all occupations and all walks of life including the political arena and are generally very rich.

But it's not just about their money, which in itself is a king's ransom to the average worker, but the superfluous manner in which CELEBRITIES are treated by everyone as though they were ROYALTY. "CELEBRITIES" not only appear to have it all but also appear to get away with it all. Clearly, they are the "privileged" Americans.

"Teach the Children So That It Will Not Be Necessary To Teach the Adults"…Abraham Lincoln

The Progressives adopted this one quote of old Abe because it applied nicely to their indoctrination strategy which *prioritizes its targeting of children* above all others. So what exactly are our young people learning? A recent poll shows 51% of millennials reject Capitalism…33% support Socialism. Another poll revealed, "Our children now believe *white America* invented slavery and that slavery did not exist anywhere else in the world." Teachers and Professors have encapsulated "slavery" as the embodiment of our entire American History without revealing the full story.

They bypass the fact that a brutal four-year Civil War which resulted in over 700 thousand casualties, was fought by *white America to end slavery.* They conspicuously *omit* and *regard* the subsequent 13th 14th and 15th Amendments to the Constitution that (*"Abolished Slavery," "Gave Citizenship to Freed Slaves"* and the *"Right to Vote for All")* as non-events. And by ignoring these justified acts; they are denying evidence that our government... *self-corrects*. Other historical Progressive unmentionables are our World Wars and a multitude of many military conflicts whereby brave and selfless Americans *of all colors* fought and died so valiantly not only to preserve our freedoms at home but which ultimately resulted in *liberating millions of people all over the world*. Evidently, America's "generosity" and "exceptionalism" does not fare well with the Progressives' anti-American diatribe that maligns our history from its very beginnings to the present time.

Today, American History is no longer mandatory in our classrooms. History majors at George Washington University are no longer required to take a U.S. history course in order to graduate. In other words, it is now possible to receive a history degree from George Washington University without studying history.*

The Progressive Democrats are expunging America's history out of existence because their business is to kill off America and they want no tell-tale evidence left behind. Their exclusive blueprint for the reinvention of America needs to be from the ground up so burn the history books and remove all monuments and statues that reveal and tell the true story of our unique American history.

"Whoever Controls the Language Controls You"...
George Orwell

The Progressive movement is very mindful and deliberate with their choice of words. They choose their words the way a warrior chooses his weapons because *their words are their weapons* in this ideological warfare they have waged on America. Meritorious hook words like *fairness, inclusive and tolerance* were all analytically chosen to entice people into their radical objectives and are not indicative of the word's intended definition. *"Politically Correct" and "Offensive"* are powerful *regulator* words that put restrictions on *freedom of speech* that could otherwise thwart an oppressive dictatorial agenda.

A few years back, the "go to word" was DIVERSITY. President Obama's proclamation that America was *not* DIVERSIFIED enough was yet another head-scratcher. Hard to process a concept that the United States is *not diversified* when our citizenry is comprised of every nationality, race, religion and culture in existence and adopts a Constitution and a Rule of Law that is applicable to all. Yet *"diversity" (like politically correct)* when applied accordingly is now the operative word entrenched in all our learning institutions throughout the nation and is constantly being jammed down our student's throats unless, of course, it is *diversity of thought.* In that case, Academia's exclusively owned diversified system is neither inclusive nor tolerant on anything that strays from their *specific* ideology.

Academia's premise emphatically implies "people of color" are disadvantaged because "white people" are the only beneficiaries of a free and competitive government. Hence, this packaged assault in the name of "*diversity*" is two-fold. It not only indicts the "white race" but implicates *Capitalism, Competition* and *America* in general as obstacles that prevent "students of color" from succeeding. This further promotes a philosophy of *inclusion by exclusion as* Whites, Conservatives and American Patriots are now on the Progressive hit list.

A group of students at Evergreen University recently put forth an event in which all *white* students, *white* professors and *white* faculty members were informed to *not attend* the university for "A Day without White People." Only one professor rejected this action and he was immediately scorned and confronted by a hostile mob of students who swiftly labeled him as a "racist." The faculty agreed with the students. Today, the professor is an outcast.

Diversity classes and seminars are now replacing many traditional subjects. Wayne State University overhauled class requirements and have dumped "*math*" for *Diversity classes.** Bing Hampton University offers training classes on *White Superiority* and the *Privileged White*.* Two major public Universities are now offering classes on *The Problem of Whiteness*.* Yale University claims English classes focus mostly on *white male writers* like Shakespeare, Milton, etc. and want to do away with studies of writers who are *pre 18th century*.* In a Middle School in California, the Principal would not release the results of a School Council election *that all students voted on* because the winners were *white and* were not *diverse* enough. This teaching moment taught her students *bigotry* is necessary and acceptable when it applies to WHITE FOLKS.*

A "Professor" from Drexel University took to his twitter account just ahead of Christmas to issue this tweet, "All I want for Christmas is White Genocide." *

These reported incidents are just a small sampling of the messaging and unchallenged harrowing ideology being taught throughout our primary and higher educational school system on a daily basis. So where is the "offensive" outcry from anyone?

(FIX THIS NATION.COM printed the following :)

"Documentary filmmaker Whitney Dow made a film series called the "Whiteness Project" that involves interviewing white millennials about the nature of their race. The filmmaker believes the grand theory that white people are the beneficiaries of invisible "Privilege." Not surprisingly, white millennials embraced their own demonization. Liberals have successfully convinced millions of white Americans to feel ashamed of themselves - not for anything they did, but merely for being born into an "oppressive" society. At its core, this actually has nothing to do with race. It's just one more trick Liberals are using to encourage Americans to hate their own country. Without that motivation, the Socialist Revolution will never happen."

In the 18th Century, Charles de Secondat wrote "A government should be set up so that: *No man need be afraid of another.*"

Those words should be a *no-brainer for all governments to acknowledge and incorporate;* but many do not. *And these days it appears many "woke" Americans (especially the young) create and THRIVE on "fear of another" so as to self-identify as a victim. Victimhood is now an aspiration not a tragedy.*

Unfortunately, this type of messaging is running rampant in America and obviously it is neither prudent nor constructive to relive mistakes from our past as if those same horrific mistakes such as *slavery* were never self-corrected and still exist today. That false "teaching moment" concept only keeps young minds stuck in the PAST; steals their PRESENT and eliminates any FUTURE endeavors. Regarding our educational system; it is time to re-construct our entire public school system by allowing school choice, *elaborating* on historical events, revamping our school's text books and curriculums and re-examining our teachers' priorities… quickly and diligently.

"The Ends Justify the Means"…Niccolo Machiavelli (1469-1527)

Mass illegal immigration was encouraged and enhanced by the Obama Administration throughout his tenure of the past 8 years even though the United States welcomes *one million legal immigrants* to our shores every year. Many do not buy the "humanitarian" explanation for this ambiguous importation of illegals to our country. Some say the real objective was to build a stronger Democrat voting bloc. Others feel it was a strategy to reduce the population of "whites" by increasing our population with *"people of color"* since the massive importation of individuals induced to come here are *people of color*. This would suggest the Democrat's interest to alter the demography of our country is detrimental in their quest to reinvent America to their liking.

On January 29, 2016, former Attorney General Eric Holder used a criminal justice conference to settle some scores with political rivals with whom he clashed. Regarding voter ID and immigration laws, Holder refers to the issue in starkly political terms. He observed that elements of the country are unsettled by the major demographic changes taking place under the OBAMA COALITION, pointing out that *the United States will no longer be majority white by 2043*. Was that the strategy and intended goal of the OBAMA COALITION?

"The Goal of Socialism is Communism"...Vladmir Lenin (Leader of the Soviet Revolution)

Only in America can both friend and foe alike share our freedoms equally to further their cause for both righteous and nefarious outcomes. Our contemptible foes rigorously *utilize* and *depend* on the very freedoms they mean to obliterate and abolish in the future if they have their way. Regrettably, they are having their way as our American schooled millennials continue to gravitate toward *Socialism over Capitalism*. They continue to believe they will have the same freedoms afforded them in a Democracy if Socialism prevails because no one is telling them otherwise.

No one is telling them to check out Venezuela who also made that same choice not too long ago when they sold out to Socialism and are now left with *nothing...* except buyer's remorse. No one is telling them because these days our precious and priceless "*freedom of speech and thought*" is selectively and methodically being shut down, shut out and censured from many important information and messaging venues and platforms throughout the country. Silicon Valley is now a *cultural power* that is taking over journalism. Unfortunately, social media's machines (Google, Face Book, Twitter and Instagram) have to be extreme left wing. Once again, it's this denial of our basic freedoms *on all things* that should enlighten everyone as to what America would look like (*a Fascist single party system*) if these Socialist Democrat ideologues were granted total control of our country.

As stated earlier, "diversity" of all things is the name of the game but not all institutions can withstand this subjective scrutiny. A country's culture is what distinguishes one country from another and every country has its own culture and values. Case in point; In America, we revere our dogs while in some cultures, they eat their dogs. In some countries, cows are sacred but in America, we eat cows. In some patriarchy cultures, "Honour Killings" are acceptable but in America; it's against the law, etc. etc. And so it goes. Therefore, even though we are a multi diversified country regarding our population, we still have a structural American Culture that is clear and benevolent and must prevail. If other countries' cultures are not compatible or in harmony with our culture; we cannot allow "diversity" to even be an issue. Destroying our American Culture just to appease a radical cultural revolution in the name of diversity would only lead to ambiguity, chaos and violence.

In 1777, Frenchman Marquis de Lafayette sailed to the newly declared United States to fight in the American Revolutionary War so that *"Liberty would have a country."* Today, that country is losing its *"Liberty"* to a contrary political ideology and anti-American culture.

The radical leaders of an anti-American Revolutionary Movement who favor *Socialism, Communism* or even *global governance over a Free Trade Democracy* lost a crucial election that stopped them from finalizing a fast-moving dangerous agenda. This leftist movement has been infiltrating, indoctrinating, propagandizing and methodically chipping away at our system of governing within all our institutions since the 1960's but were never so blatantly emboldened until Barack Obama endorsed and validated them. Orchestrated chaos can destroy any country. For these anarchists who have come so far, this Presidential loss was an unthinkable scenario.

Subsequently, *they will not go gentle into that good night*...but neither can we. We have to confront violent and intimidating actions wherever it strikes and *stop normalizing anarchy.* Webster's New World Dictionary defines *intimidation* as "to make afraid, as with threats." The radical left is using *mob intimidation* as their primary weapon to win their ideology war against America. They are *intimidating (a threatening tactic)* all those they oppose; whether it's the lone person on the street, small businesses, big corporations, politicians or anyone else in between. Essentially, they are *scaring us into submission.* It is now time to call out and stop all forms of *intimidation* with strong ramifications and accountability.

There is no difference between a foreign enemy who is hell-bent on destroying our way of life and home grown citizens with the same mindset. Our *"Individual Freedom"* and *"Free Will"* are non-negotiable. There are no exceptions, substitutes or alternatives... period. God willing, there will be no Socialist *Reinvention of America*...but if America fails; We will indeed become *the huddled masses yearning to be free.**

ABOUT THE AUTHOR

Born and schooled in Orange, New Jersey and New York City. After attending one year of Jr. College, family moved to Hollywood, California where she lived for 10 years before moving to Washington, DC where she still resides.

Has worked as an accounting assistant and freelance editor in various venues and had "Memories" (a poem) and "Thoughts on Words" (a paperback) published. Won 1st place trophy in the "American Open Chess Tournament" women's category.

Has been involved with politics since her childhood as her father who was very active in local politics always encouraged her and her sister to volunteer their services wherever needed but particularly to various local political elections.

Has continued to work on countless political campaigns as a volunteer and worked eight years at the White House EOB under President Reagan's Administration. She passionately takes the position that "Politics and your destiny are synonymous" because LIBERTY is everything.*